Seon Master Man Gong's Dharma Talks

The Gateless Gate

Seon Master Man Gong's Dharma Talks

Preface

This book, 『Seon Master Man Gong's Dharma Talks』 , the content is not long, but it contains deep Seon-Wisdom of a very pithy remark, and it has been widely read especially by Seon practitioners.

The book that is combinded together is Seon Master Mu Mun(1183~1260)'s 『The Gateless Gate』 . It contains only 48 Hwadus, but no other preface or epilogue is included.

I will replace the introduction with Mu Mun's self-preface which is written in the preface of 『The Gateless Gate』 .

The Great Way has no gate.
Though the path has a thousand branches,
Once you pass through this barrier,
You confidently stride across the universe.

Editor   palms together

※   『Seon Master Man Gong's Dharma Talks』 has been edited and translated by referring to previous translated book, 『The Teachings of Zen Master Man Gong, 2009』 . 『The Gateless Gate』 has been also edited and translated by referring to various translated books.

I wouldn't have been able to edit or translate these books without this previous translated books.

Contents

An appendix

Chapter *I*. **What Am I? The Necessity of Finding Your True Self**

1. It is said that human beings are the most precious of all things because they can attain their true nature.

2. True nature means total freedom, being in charge of one's life, yet human beings are rarely free any time or place. They cannot control their lives because their deluded self becomes the boss while their true nature is just a slave.

3. The deluded self is the offspring of true nature. The mind we are currently using is just incorrect mind that arises from deluded self. True nature (clear mind or bodhisattva mind) is correct mind, which has no beginning and no end; it has no existence or extinction, yet it lacks nothing.

4. How is a human being who has lost sight of his true nature(true I) any different from an animal which only pursues sex and food

instinctively? No matter how great or famous you are, if you do not attain your true nature, you are just like a molecule, subject to the four types of birth and death and the six realms of existence (samsara).

5. In our world most people live together, sharing a lifestyle, mindlessly following their karma. Their lives just happen, without direction. They don't see the terrifying thing waiting for them. When death comes, they are blind to what lies ahead.

6. If I shout someone's name and they immediately answer, "Yes!" – that is true nature. True nature has no birth or death. It can't catch fire, get wet, or be cut with a knife. It is completely free and without hindrance.

7. Just like the prisoner screaming as he is dragged, twisting behind a horse, we are being dragged down the road of suffering by the chains of karma. Repeatedly, we follow the cycles of life,

sickness, old age and death. Only your wisdom sword can cut these chains.

8. No matter how well educated or respected they are, if they don't know about finding their true self, they are like person who have lost their mind.

9. When Sakyamuni Buddha was born, he pointed with one hand to the sky and the other to the ground and said, "Between the heavens above and the earth below, only 'I' am holy." This 'I' means the true nature.

10. Everyone already has Buddha nature (true nature) but they cannot become Buddha because they do not understand themselves.

11. Everything is 'I'(true nature). If you apply effort to anything else other than finding it, even the smallest effort, is a waste.

12. Everyone has three bodies: a physical body, a karma body and a dharma body. When

these three bodies function as one body, they become a true human being.

13. All action originates from the dharma body. Since the dharma body is not separate from the physical body or the karma body, all phenomena in themselves are just the dharma body beyond life and death.

14. The place beyond life and death includes both the sentient and the non-sentient. Therefore, all the weapons of the universe cannot destroy the true nature of even one blade of grass.

15. In our world, there is a lot of teaching about how to find and understand our true nature. These are all just the understanding of the discrimination-consciousness from the point of view of our karma. Our true nature is inconceivable and beyond imagination.

16. True nature(true I) is an indestructible diamond body which cannot die. Beyond time, it has endless life. Each life and death of the form

body is just like changing clothes; the true person is able to take off and wear the clothes of life and death freely.

17. The knowledge you get through seeing and listening will not lead to the attainment of your true nature. Thinking about true nature is already not true nature.

18. True nature can be only found in the realm of no-thought because the realm of no-thought contains all existence and is already complete.

19. If a person attains final enlightenment while having the Buddha as a goal then one will find that they themselves are the Buddha. After all, I must find myself in me.

Chapter II. Seon Practice: The Way to Find Your True Nature

1. In our world there is no place to find your true self, nor a teacher to show you how. Only in a Seon-room(where Seon practitioners practice) in Buddhism can we learn the right way to find our true nature.

2. Seon practice means that everyone studies to get back their own mind. This is most urgent.

3. The study of worldly knowledge only serves this temporary life from the delusion of my body. But Seon study leads to a wisdom which is beyond time and space, beyond our body, and even beyond this life.

4. The Seon-room(or Seon-hall) is not the only Seon-room. For those who practice Seon, their own body is also a Seon-room. You can practice Seon nonstop, when you are standing, walking, sitting or lying down–even when you are silent or speaking.

This means that one can always stay in the Seon-room.

5. You can never practice Seon alone. You shouldn't leave your teacher because only they can teach you, without hindrance, not only about life's concerns but also about all problems.

6. It is very difficult to hear even one word from a Seon teacher. It may only happen once in ten thousand kalpas. If you hear this one word and attain it, you can realize your true nature without practicing Seon.

7. Listening to a Dharma speech is like walking on thin ice; you must be very focused and sincere.

8. 'Seon Master' is not just a conventional title like doctor or teacher. They have mastered the principles of the universe and inherited a lineage of wisdom from the Buddhas and eminent teachers.

9. Principle and phenomena are part of one circle. No matter where you start, you will attain your goal. But, you cannot attain your true nature without a Seon Master's teaching.

10. Listening to a Seon Master's teaching without believing or acting on it will result in bad karma. Such casual disregard will make it difficult for you to ever hear this kind of teaching again.

11. The more that you believe in your Seon teacher, the more you will attain.

12. Anyone who knows that soy sauce is salty can practice Seon.

13. The reason that you have difficulties practicing Seon is because in your previous life you just played around. When you pay your debt for this, then you can get a result.

14. If you have great faith without doubt, your foundation for practicing the Dao is already strong.

15. When great faith, great courage and great question become one, then you can succeed in your practice.

16. If you have complete faith, then your Samadhi energy get matched with objects, and you can function correctly in any situation without hindrance.

17. If your mind is not touched by the Dharma speech, it will be very difficult for you to get a human body again.

18. A practicing person should first try to find a good teacher; after completing your practice, your obligation is to teach others.

19. The biggest sin of all is calling yourself a Seon Master and teaching others without authority from a keen-eyed lineage holder.

20. Dharma can only be found when language stops and mind is cut off. Dharma is inherited only through mind to mind transmission.

Without a teacher's direct instruction, Dharma cannot be learned.

21. The basis of practice depends on practitioner's a great inspirit of the earnest aspiration to attain enlightenment. Practice has no particular limits. However, it is best to begin in your twenties.

22. Seon practice is not an ordinary study or learning. It points to something outside the usual concept of what it means to study, because this way or path has no opposites. One should attain in the realm where is no room for even the tip of a single hair.

23. The result of one hundred years of worldly study cannot match the attainment of one moment in the realm of no-thought.

24. All sentient beings have the feeling of attraction to the opposite sex from birth, become habituated to the principle of sexual yinyang, lifetime after lifetime. The greatest hindrance to

focusing one's mind is reasoning(thinking) in terms of opposites. It is most important that practicing people stay away from the opposite sex.

25. Though you put down all things and keep one mind, when you take one more step in the realm of no-thought where even the thought of one mind is forgotten, you can find your true nature.

26. The small 'I' must be extinguished. Until I achieve the result of practice, I must get rid of the 'I' to the extent that I become like a rotten stump and never look back.

27. There are three conditions which are necessary for me to find my true self: I) a practicing place, ii) a teacher and iii) a Dharma friend.

28. One must follow the way with sincerity and integrity. Even though there are slightly different teaching styles, the Way is one. If

you are not sincere you will be wasting your time and suffer a mental loss.

29. You need a teacher to make something as simple as straw sandals. Even the common mushroom has its own place to grow. So, how could anyone who wants to attain the Way, which includes everything, not to have a teacher? How can there not be a special place for a person of the Way who has made universal energy their own? The influence of Dharma friends is stronger than a teacher's teaching.

30. If you practice Seon and resolve life's great question then all your bad actions and sins for many lives will be extinguished, and you will end the suffering of samsara.

31. While you are practicing, give up your function as a human being: become deaf, blind and stupid (not clever). If you don't attach to anything then the big 'I' appears by itself.

32. The practice of Seon has existed for a long time. In the last one thousand and five hundred years, eminent teachers developed a Seon practice based on the great question, which produced numberless teachers. There are one thousand and seven hundred Gong-ans. When I first started practicing, I took up the question, "The myriad things return to One, where does the One return to?" This Gong-an has two levels. The best question for a beginner is, "The myriad things return to One, what is the One?" Even though you keep questioning, when you enter a clear and calm realm of no-thought where even the thought of questioning has been cut off, you will see your true nature.

33. The One neither exists nor does it not exist. It is not spirit, soul, or mind. Then what is it? As you question, keep your mind like a cat, single-mindedly watching a mouse. The question should be like water flowing, nonstop. If you keep the question sincerely, you will find the One, someday.

34. You will have great difficulty practicing Seon if you regret leaving behind worldly study and pride or if you are attached to some special talent. So, you should return to being a blank page.

35. If you can pay the price of a very restrictive practice, you will get great freedom.

36. In the old days there used to be people who would suddenly forget about life and death with just one word from a Seon teacher. Also, there were many people who got enlightenment after three or seven days with just one word from a Seon teacher. However, people these days have very little patience and practice Seon as a sideline. Because of this, people who have practiced for even twenty or thirty years still have not attained Buddhism's great meaning.

37. When you eat rice yourself, you feel full. If you don't practice Seon yourself, even the Buddha and eminent teachers cannot help you.

38. If you want to practice Seon, you must first calm down the battle of the six senses and stabilize your mind, that's when you're ready to study.

39. Seon practice is the most free and easiest study, the practitioners who are practicing this Seon study can avoid being noticed by even the emissaries of the kingdom of hell.

40. When one thought appears, everything appears. When one thought disappears, everything disappears. The appearance and disappearance of my one thought is the creation and destruction of the whole universe, the life and death of life.

41. The teaching phrase, "If you open your mouth, it's already a mistake!" points to the mind before name and form.

42. When you feel that your practice is going well, it has already gone wrong.

43. Experience Seon practice in a dream and make it a teacher for Seon practice.

44. Even in a deep dreamless sleep you should know where you put your mind.

45. Dreaming is the function of karma body. When awake, people wander through life controlled by thinking. In Dreams, it is to imitate the actions of form body by the function of karma body.

46. You should be able to practice as if dreaming and awake are one.

47. Can you keep your consistent mind even if your body is being burned by fire? If you decide you can't do that, know that when you pass from life to death, your future path will be dark and you won't know what to do.

48. A practicing person should do the practice of non-practice. Not to practice is more difficult than to practice.

49. Rather than worry about how well I am practicing, I have to build up decisive faith that there is nothing to do except this practice.

50. The practitioner must overcome the pitfall of death once both before and after enlightenment.

51. Seon practice is like a blast furnace that melts all karmic obstacles and habitual energy.

52. Although you have to be compassionate when treating people, when it comes to your own practice, you must be brutally uncompromising; otherwise you will never defeat the eighty-four thousand illusions of mind.

53. Just before their execution, a person may have some thinking but during practice, one should not mix in even the slightest glimmer of a thought.

54. During practice, the sleep demon should be more feared than deluded thinking. So, you must first bring this demon to it's knees.

55. It is extremely difficult to get a human body, so don't miss this opportunity to get the human body, and practice hard. Once you miss this chance it will be very difficult to get it again.

56. If you don't attain strength in your practice, only your human karma will remain when you die. At this time, even animals can appear to you as handsome men and women, leading you to an animal realm in your next life.

57. The time of a person practicing Seon is of the utmost importance, so don't waste even one moment.

58. You are the most free and relaxed when using the toilet. If you get into one mind, even at that time you can get enlightenment.

59. The reason the achievement of practice is delayed is because we always think that we have more time. When you wake up in the morning, you should always say to yourself, "I am still alive – I did not die. I should finish this great work. There is no tomorrow."

60. At night when you lie down to sleep, think about how much you practiced that day. If you spent more time thinking and sleeping than practice, then you should strongly urge yourself to practice more everyday and do it!

61. If illusions or sleep appear during practice, then recall that in this life you have not been free from life and death. This will help refresh your mind.

62. If you have even the smallest thought of self-concern when you die, then even the memory of practicing Seon will disappear.

63. Since you become a monk(nun) who has left home to get out of samsara, if you do

anything other than keeping to the way of practicing Seon, it will only be what you strengthen the habits of life and death.

64. If you practice Seon thinking that you will get something special, you will fall into heresy.

65. Even though a person who's gotten the way performs various supernatural acts and shows mysterious miracles, it is all merely characteristics of the Dharma, one should never go down this path.

66. Faith is a stepping stone towards Buddha. Stepping this faith that has no 'I', going beyond the Buddha, we must find our own true nature.

67. A Seon practitioner should behave like one – don't be frivolous, so a Seon practitioner should be able to teach others without opening one's mouth.

68. There are four stages of attainment in practice: i) Knowing that there is no life or death, ii) Being in accord with the fact that there is no life or death, iii) Attaining no life or death, iv) Using the fact that there is no life or death without hindrance. Only when you attain fourth stages, you will be a great and free person who has no hindrance in both the cosmic law and the world of phenomena.

69. Don't try to understand anything during practice. If you attain strength in your practice, enlightenment will appear by itself.

70. If you become lazy in your practice because you think that you have gotten something, even the affinity with the Buddha Dharma can disappear.

71. The mind that does not rely on material, in the place that has no shape, can be realized through all actions.

72. Mind creates the material world but the existence and function of mind appears through the material.

73. Each thing in the material world has a function specified by its name. Mind has no name or form but is the source of all existence. Everyone already has the Mind which possesses an infinite capacity to accomplish anything. If you return to this Mind, you can do anything.

74. In the theatre of the mind, Two actors, 'life and death' and 'good and bad', are in turn directing the tragicomedy of an infinite forms in front of the background of the universe.

75. No matter how advanced civilization's country is, if there is no a person of the Way, it is a country that lacks substance. No matter how poor the country is, if there is a person of the Way, it is a country that does not lack substance.

76. A person of the Way should not be a person of the Way who is nothing more than a

pronoun of a person of the Way. Ultimately practitioner must attain the place before name and form, leave the idol called 'a people of the Way', escape from the constraints of precepts or practice and become a completely independent person. At that time the practitioner can come and go freely in the six states of karmic existence and escape suffering.

Chapter *III*.   Human Life

1. A human being's life is no more than a short act in a play. When one scene of this play ends, our consciousness, which makes happiness, anger, sadness and pleasure, disappear without a trace. The flesh dissolves into rot. What kind of impermanent thing is this? Also, did you experience even one second of freedom during this brief moment of impermanence? Even while eating, if an unexpected death occurs, you can't swallow the rice you chewed and die, and even if you spend a lot of money to build a house, if you suddenly encounter a fire, you can't even sit inside the room once and become in vain. Even in my own life, I always lose my freedom in this way. How absurd it is to establish a society and a nation that are groups of life!, isn't it sad? If you want true freedom, you must know its basis. People may clamor for freedom, but if they don't know its source, it is like talking about eating well without having any rice.

2. People know the world of dream and phantasma, the reflection of own karma body, as the real world, and live by crying and laughing. It is like a ginkgo tree that sees its own reflection in a pond and thinks that it has found a mate and then bears fruit.

3. Human life is not just a continuation of this life but a continuation of birth and extinction over and over again. Humans forget the moment of death, forget all about the life before and after death, and cannot remember the suffering that enters into the womb and the suffering at birth. They only think about their present life through the limited understanding provided by the six consciousnesses. Visiting heaven and hell, having a human or animal body – all these lives come and go very fast. Just like a movie, the scenes pass by quickly.

4. Our life cannot bring back the past nor guarantee the future. There is only the present. When we have a complete grasp of this present,

we can colligate the past, present and future, live a unified life of the past, present and future.

5. To live means only living in the present , not in the past and not in the future. The present is a moment of passing between the past and the future which never stops flowing. In this moment you may feel life is not stable – this is not true life! There is a reality where the past and the present merge, it is because the present is the future of the past and also the past of the future, therefore past, present and future is one.

6. Centering on this world in which we live, above, there are countless worlds of the best unimaginable culture; Below is the inferior and heinous world, whose quantity and number cannot be counted; Since both of these worlds are dreamlike and phantasmal worlds, Which one is the true world? To find the answer to this question is to attain the world of true self.

7. Our present life is the whole world. If you don't get satisfaction in this life, you will not get it anywhere.

8. Every human being wants something good out of life but nobody understands that this wanting is the source of suffering.

9. The major contents of one's life: old age, sickness, death, happiness, anger, sadness and pleasure are just a gathering and a result of foolish habits learned in many lives. When we realize it clearly, we can get out of life and death.

10. Numberless kinds of sentient beings are packed in this universe, each forming their own societies. As a result of the habits of many life times, our six consciousnesses become more and more fixed. Human beings cannot see or feel beyond these limitations so they have no way of understanding sentient beings of other realms. Heavenly beings and hell, gods and ghosts are the name and form of numberless kinds of sentient

beings that we can't judge by our six consciousness -es.

11. Each person's character is the product of habit. Genius and talent are the product of such habits over many lifetimes. Your karma is your habit.

12. Things are always combining and dissolving. The universe is created and extinguished over and over again through infinite time. The same is true of our lives; life is that repeats birth and death.

13. Sentient beings (humans, animals, worms etc.) have limited, self-centered lives controlled by their small 'I'. Having lost their freedom they are dragged around by their karma, wandering through the six realms of existence and reappearing through the four kinds of birth. Buddhas make the whole universe their own by becoming one with it. All sentient beings are the Buddha's body and the three thousand worlds are the Buddha's home.

Buddhas are totally free to occupy or leave any body or home.

14. Since Buddhas have made the whole universe their own, they can freely use the form and function of whole universe.

15. Everyone thinks heaven is the best place to go to and hell is where we shouldn't go, but actually the whole universe is just one body; heaven and hell are one home. Sentient beings are always splitting their world into two. They can even divide their bodies into two parts, sending one part to heaven and the other to hell according to their karmic affinities.

16. Anyone whose character is controlled by their situation can not attain eternal peace.

17. Because ordinary people consider this bag of blood and excrement their true body, they think that hot, cold, thirst and hunger are the only important considerations. There is no way for these people to get out of the suffering of samsara.

18. The perceptions created through the six consciousnesses (eyes, ears, nose, tongue, body and mind) are always changing according to time and circumstance. How can we possibly grasp the original nature of life using these six consciousness -es?

19. Even though there are very advanced and profound worldly theories, they cannot solve your life's problems because all these theories are attached to name and form.

20. If there is a teaching that enlightens you to what theory cannot explain, then this teaching is the great teacher to guide to the doorway to the Dao.

21. Those who talk about metaphysics and idealism are not aware that they themselves are not free from the material world.

22. In the whole world there is no one who speaks correctly or incorrectly.

23. Even though god presides freely, using supernatural power over the fortunes of human beings, it is nothing but the devil without a body.

24. Those who deny the existence of god cannot escape stupidity; those who believe in god cannot avoid ignorance.

25. Human beings are proud of the infinite ability of modern science. However, if they use it incorrectly, it will create more harm than good. Only when this world become the age of true science that the egotism of both me and others disappears, and mind and matter become one, all human beings can live a stable life under a reasonable system. True peace will come when a spiritual culture based on true nature is established in their mind by every human being.

26. We cannot subdue all of nature with the power of science, only part of it. Even if we could subdue it, it would just be the result of our human habits. We still would not have overcome our habits. Only after we have completely controlled

our habits and mastered the essence can we use nature and our habits freely.

27. The scientist whose mind and the material world have become one is able to display his infinite ability forever.

28. Since people these days are proud and nervous, when they listen to a Dharma talk which they don't understand, they don't listen carefully, and they enjoy refuting its content without any reason or grounds. By doing this they go down a dark path.

29. Egoistic attachment is an exclusive spirit. It is ignorance that reduces me more and more because I do not know that others are me.

30. Sentient beings know that they must do well and be good. But they don't realize that they must find the self which makes them do well and be good.

31. People say that human beings are the most precious of all beings because they have the ability to think and speculate. Yet, they don't even try to understand what thinking and speculation are.

32. Even though sentient beings don't know their true selves at all, some pretend to be scholars or religious leaders, discussing life's great questions. This is like killing life while trying to save it.

33. If we take even one step beyond theory and scholarly study, then we can find our true self. Life's great questions cannot be solved before we find our true self.

34. Life's great questions cannot be solved through hope or by accidental encounters for the answer of these questions. When people attain one's true self, then one can freely deal with life both in theory and your daily actions (karma).

35. Sentient beings only know how to know; they don't know how to 'don't know'.

36. If you know this 'don't know', then you truly know. The way of truly knowing is knowing how to not know. Just then one attains one's true nature.

37. We are like brothers born of the same womb (mother earth) confronting each other with guns and swords. Who are we really going to kill by sharpening our swords? Who are we really killing by making arms? This is the human tragedy.

Chapter IV. **Buddha Dharma**

1. If you say 'Buddha Dharma', already that is not Buddha Dharma.

2. Everything, as it is, is Buddha Dharma. If you get up on a soapbox to preach about the Buddha Dharma, the meaning is already lost.

3. Material things are to be used; Mind is the basis. When Mind and the material become one, this is the Buddha Dharma. Unless the Buddha Dharma is fully fulfilled, life's eternal happiness is not guaranteed.

4. Buddha Dharma is appropriate for any historical period or human circumstance.

5. Even after listening the Buddha Dharma, if the center of life does not touched, then this person has already lost human status.

6. Buddha is Mind; Dharma is the material. Before the Buddha Dharma appeared as name and form and even before the historical Buddha appeared, true nature existed. If one puts down the 'I', which is like a piece of unglazed pottery, then one will get a Dharma body which is like the vessel of seven treasures. (gold, silver, lapis, crystal, coral, agate and pearl).

7. It is not the mouth which speaks; it is not the hand which works. When you find the one who really speaks and works, then you will become an authentic human who can truly speak and work.

8. Buddha Dharma is responsible for the body and the mind. How anxious is life without someone in charge! Once you realize this you will return to the Buddha Dharma immediately.

9. Worldly principles and the Buddha Dharma are not two. Buddha and sentient beings are one. When you attain this teaching of non-duality, you will become a true person.

10. Even a common worldly person, if he(she) knows the Buddha Dharma, he(she) is a monk(nun). Even a monk(nun), if a monk(nun) doesn't know the Buddha Dharma, the monk(nun) is a common worldly person.

11. To open different locks you need many kinds of keys. If you want to comprehend the numberless obscure principles of samadhi, you will need ten thousand wisdom keys.

12. Denying the Buddha Dharma is denying oneself. If you reject the Buddha Dharma, you reject yourself, because you are the Buddha.

13. Every sound is a Dharma talk and everything is the true body of the Buddha. But we always hear that it is very difficult to encounter the Buddha Dharma even once in ten million kalpas. This puzzling situation deserves our serious consideration.

Chapter *V*. **Buddhism**

1. If you defend your theory of Buddhism, you are already going against its basic tenets because Buddhism's principles are beyond egoism.

2. The fundamental meaning of Buddhism does not punish the bad or encourage the good because both good and bad are the Buddha Dharma. The pleasures of heaven and the suffering of hell are all created by oneself.

3. Nothing can be gotten without paying a price and there is no success without effort. This is the basic principle of the universe.

4. Everything itself is Buddha so there can be no fixed rules or basic organization for teaching. Buddhism is taught according to character and circumstances.

5. The theory of Mind-only in Buddhism is not the opposite of materialism. It is a absolute Mind-only where mind and matter are non-duality.

6. Space (true nature) gives birth to mind; mind gives birth to personality, which gives birth to action.

7. Usually people think that the terms, 'matter' and 'mind' completely explain the basic nature of the universe. However, the true nature of the universe lies somewhere else.

8. In Buddhism, the Dharma body is beyond spirit and the true human is beyond the soul. Attaining this is final enlightenment. The Dharma body is the root of the form body, spirit and soul. When the form body, spirit and soul lose their root, they merely move through life, continu- ally replacing each other(samsara). This is the human being in this secular world.

9. Buddhism is an educational institution which completes the true nature of all human beings.

Other religions, too, are a kind of bridge and process to complete the true self.

10. The deep meaning of Buddhism doctrine cannot be expressed in words; however, because each one has Buddha-nature, it is possible to transmit it from mind to mind. A teacher can not teach it nor can a student be taught. Giving it and receiving it are not possible. But this Dharma is inherited by the Buddhas of the past and the future.

Chapter VI. **Monks and Nuns**

1. Monastics refer to a person before name and form appear. They are the host for all beings, teaching even those in heaven.

2. Monastics, whose life is to practice, must give up their families (parents, mates and children), all their possessions and even themselves.

3. Monastics should not let their lives be controlled by fate. They should have nothing to do with the kingdom of hell, and their happiness or unhappiness should not be dependent on others.

4. Monastic discipline means keeping your true nature pure as a white lotus — don't attach to worldly things.

5. The completion of even worldly study can take half a lifetime, so how can we say it is boring to study for ten thousand years to find the way to infinite life?

6. Many feel the need for worldly educa- tion which isn't concerned with the wheel of life and death; imagine how much more we need the lessons of Seon practice, which cut the hold of life and death forever and allow us to realize our true nature. Therefore this is the most important thing that must be known urgently to all mankind.

7. Worldly people adopt the law as a 'doing', but monastics(monks and nuns) adopt the law as a 'non-doing'.

8. Worldly people do everything with attachment, while monastics act through cutting attachment. Monastics should not even attach to Buddha or patriarchs.

9. The inheritance of worldly people is through blood lines, while the inheritance of monastics is through the enlightened mind, which is the Dao. The biggest sin for a worldly person is to interrupt the inheritance from their ancestors. For monastics, who are the students of the

Buddha, there is no greater sin than not inheriting the Dharma.

10. In ancient times, older laywomen who understood the Dharma would often test monks. But these days, even monks who should lead assemblies do not understand the Buddha Dharma. This is truly a time of darkness. How can the people not fall into a difficult and miserable state!

11. The fortune and misfortune of mankind are the result of ups and downs of Buddhism.

12. World peace always goes together with the flourishing of Buddhism.

13. The tattered clothes of practicing sunims (monks and nuns) are very precious, even the clothes of a king cannot compare. The clothes of a king cover a lot of bad karma but a sunim's tattered clothes take away karma and allow wisdom to grow.

14. If a monastic still envies a layperson's wealth and fame or is lonely and still fells sorrow, it is truly shameful.

15. A monastic is a person who has attained becoming one with the universe.

16. Monastics should not use anything for themselves even if it is gained through their own efforts, because everything they have is the property of the Three Jewels (Buddha, Dharma and Sangha).

17. If you receive an offering as a monastic and use it without practicing, you are a swindler.

18. If you are a monastic and do not function correctly, you sin against your family, country and sangha.

19. If a person becomes a monastic when they are young, before their true nature is tainted, and they function correctly their whole life, then

the virtue that they create will cover both heaven and earth.

20. There are many monastics who waste lay people's offerings and don't practice sincerely. Because of this there are very few lay people these days to support monastic life. The effort that one makes for the Dao becomes the Dao, so you must practice bravely, even in very difficult situations.

21. The direction of your thoughts is determined only through practice. When you are able to choose the direction of your thoughts, then you can take the correct path and infinite life is guaranteed.

22. Worldly life allows for lapses of attention, but monastic life requires that practice be continuous, even in a dream. Even a small gap allows all kinds of hindrances to appear.

23. Even a murderer of ten million people who repents, pays homage to the Buddha and becomes a practicing monk, can take away the hatred

of his victims and remove the bad karma they have created for infinite kalpas.

24. Because people attach to the deluded self, everything they see, hear and do become impermanent.

25. Sentient beings cannot escape the samsara of the six realms controlled by time and space because they are attached to living only in time and space.

Chapter VII. Rules for living in the Sangha

1. Monks and nuns must live with the sangha and consider it a treasure.

2. Monastics should not create factions within the sangha. If one makes distinctions like 'us' then you have already violated the spirit of the sangha.

3. Monastics should leave behind the human world based on material values and live in a spiritually based community where you and I become one.

4. Serving the sangha is serving Buddha.

5. Having cut off their affinity for worldly living, monastics should respect each other as they clean their karma. They should love children and respect elders.

6. If one has already vowed to enter a student and teacher relationship, the student should respect the teacher and the teacher should lead and teach the student.

7. Monastics should first cut the mind that thinks in terms of right and wrong. If a quarrel arises you must examine yourself. If there is not your fault then just disregard it. Living this way will eliminate disputes and create peace.

8. When dealing with temple business, monastics should not be concerned with personal gain but should return the resulting acclaim or profit to the sangha.

9. Do not discuss the faults of your Dharma friend with others. If he's a true Dharma friend, then these faults are actually yours.

10. Monastics have taken on a difficult job for themselves, so always be helpful to others.

11. Mind is infinite, so too, the body, its emissary, is not limited.

12. Monastics should keep an open mind that is impartial and acts for the benefit of all.

13. Monastics should even treat insects with great love and great sadness.

14. If you gain an undeserved windfall, don't be happy because behind your gain may be the sorrow of someone else's loss.

15. The primary virtue for all monastics should be patience.

16. A monastic should be able to take all criticisms of the sangha upon themselves and be ready to give even his life for the sangha.

17. If each person does their tasks sincerely, then there will never be any disharmony within the sangha.

18. Avoiding difficulties and seeking gain from public affairs are sources of self-corruption.

19. Do not complain about being asked to dedicate yourself to something which is beyond your reach. Thinking that something is beyond your ability comes from a weakness of spirit.

Chapter VIII. **Admonitions**

1. If you inhale one breath but cannot exhale, then you are finished! You will lose your human way if you do not attain strength in your practice because your mind will not be clear when your life's light ceases.

2. Wasting time and just playing around is the source of our bad karma.

3. If you don't practice to find your true self but just chase after wealth and sex, then even if one thousand Buddhas appeared, they could not save you.

4. Even saving a small country requires a great sacrifice, so getting back your true nature demands a very large payment from you.

5. Everybody recognizes that they have lost something, but they don't know they have lost their true self.

6. If you ignore the needs of even small beings, in future you will become one of them.

7. Giving benefit to others means a true benefit to yourself. Making offerings is like opening a high interest savings account for yourself.

8. The meanest thing that you can do is to blame others for your mistake.

9. One action is better than a thousand thoughts.

10. Playing around gives rise to many kinds of danger.

11. Always act before you speak.

12. It is not the gun or knife that shoots or stabs, the real perpetrator is one's karma.

13. The scariest place is not hell, but the mind which produces anger, desire and ignorance.

14. True work is done when there is 'non-doing'. There is true goodness when one does not make compassion.

15. True speech does not come from the mouth.

16. The most frightening thing is empty space.

17. Can you show your thinking to others?

18. Have you experienced the 'bone of space'?

19. Have you seen the hair growing on a ghost's fart?

20. Can you hear the Buddha statue's Dharma speech?

21. Thinking itself is reality and the truth of existence.

22. When thinking appears, Dharma appears; when thinking disappears, all Dharmas return to emptiness.

23. Earth, wood, roof tiles and stones are themselves the Dao.

24. Suffering is the mother of Buddha.

25. You should find the Buddha in ignorance.

26. 'No mind' is the teacher of Vairocana Buddha.

27. When you cut off the desire to understand then you can understand everything, because everything is found in emptiness.

28. You should know that a scarecrow is more spiritual than a human being.

29. If you don't get anything then there is nothing to lose.

30. A useful person can not have tranquil time.

Chapter IX. **Final Words**

I have been teaching Seon students on this mountain for almost forty years. Many people come to visit me thinking they are visiting a Seon Master but they only see my form body, the house where my true nature lives. They don't see my true nature. That is not a problem but it means that they have not seen their true nature. Because they haven't seen their true nature, they cannot see their parents, siblings, wife and children, or anybody. They wander through life in vain, like a crazy person. We have to say that this is truly a world of darkness.

Dao(도, 道) is not two, but the methods of teaching Dao are different. Students who receive my teaching must do it with sincerity and dedication, not forgetting the methods I used. Ultimately, being sincere and dedicated is paying back your Dharma obligation, so you will not waste your practice or suffer a mental loss.

You should always retain three things: a place of practice, a teacher and Dharma friends.

Three thousand years after Sakyamuni Buddha, three bodhisattvas of the highest level will appear on Dok Seung mountain. Seven people of great wisdom and numberless practitioners who have attained the Way will also appear.

You should know that I am an eternal being, not dependent on a form body. Even when my Dharma speech is not heard anymore, you should still be able to see my true face that never disappears.

An appendix

1. Maha Prajna Paramita Hrdaya Sutra

Avalokitesvara Bodhisattva when practicing deeply the Prajna Paramita perceives that all five skandhas are empty and is saved from all suffering and distress. Shariputra, form does not differ from emptiness, emptiness does not differ from form. That which is form is emptiness, that which is emptiness form. The same is true of feelings, perceptions, impulses, consciousness. Shariputra, all dharmas are marked with emptiness, they do not appear or disappear, are not tainted or pure, do not increase or decrease. Therefore, in emptiness no form, no feelings, perceptions, impulses, consciousness. No eyes, no ears, no nose, no tongue, no body, no mind; no color, no sound, no smell, no taste, no touch, no object of mind; no realm of eyes and so forth until no realm of mind consciousness. No ignorance and also no extinction of it, and so forth until no old age and death and also no extinction of them. No suffering, no origination, no stopping, no path, no cognition, also no attainment with nothing to attain. The Bodhisattva depends on Prajna Paramita and the mind is no hindrance; without any hindrance no fears exist. Far apart from every perverted view one dwells in Nirvana. In the three worlds all Buddhas depend on Prajna Paramita and attain Anuttara samyak Sambodhi. Therefore, know that Prajna Paramita is the great transcendent mantra, is the great bright mantra, is the utmost mantra, is the supreme mantra, which is able to relieve all suffering and is true, not false. So proclaim the Prajna Paramita mantra, proclaim the mantra which says:

"Gate, Gate, Paragate, Parasamgate, Bodhi Svaha!"

2. The Song of Dharma-Nature

Dharma-Nature is round and interpenetrating, without the mark of duality; all dharmas are unmoving, originally still.

Without name, without characteristics, cutting off every distinction, this is understood only through enlightened wisdom, not through any other means.

True-nature is extremely profound and exceedingly subtle and sublime, it does not preserve self- nature but appears following conditions.

In one are all, in the many is one; one is all, and the many are one.

In one mote of dust is held the ten directions; and so it is, with all motes of dust.

Immeasurably long kalpas are identical to a single moment of thought; a single moment of thought is just identical to immeasurable kalpas.

The nine times and the ten times are mutually identical, yet they are not confusedly mingled and manifest separately.

The moment one first gives rise to the aspiration for awakening, it is just the moment of enlightenment.

Samsara and nirvana are always reciprocally harmonious.

Principle and phenomena are mystically without distinction,

This is the realm of all Buddhas and Bodhisattva Samantabhadra.

Ably in Ocean-Seal-Samadhi, numerous inconceivable miracles are produced according to one's wishes.

The shower of jewels benefitting beings fills all of empty space; all sentient beings obtain these benefits according to their capacities.

Therefore, when practitioners of Buddha-dharma return to the original place, it is impossible not to rest delusion (One can't help resting delusion).

Grasping unconditionally skillful means as one wishes, returning home(the primordial realm), one obtains riches according to one's capacity.

By means of the inexhaustible treasure of dharani, a true jeweled palace of Dharmadhatu is adorned.

Finally, one is seated on position of the true Middle Path, that which is originally unmoving is named Buddha.

3. Bo Wang Sam Mae Ron
(The Treasury-King's Samadhi Shastra)

1. You shouldn't seek to have no disease in your body.

    If you have no disease you come to be greedy.

    That's why the Great Sage says we should regard disease as good medicine for the body.

2. You shouldn't seek not to suffer.

    If you have no suffering you come to despise suffering and to be extravagant.

    That's why the Great Sage says we should regard suffering as a good thing in our life.

3. You shouldn't worry about hindrancesarising in your mind when you study.

    If there is no hindrance you study too much.

    That's why the Great Sage says we should regard hindrance as a good thing in our life.

4. You shouldn't seek not to encounter the evil one when you practice.

    If there is no evil your Great Vows weaken.

That's why the Great Sage says we should regard evil as a friend who helps us to keep practicing.

5. You shouldn't seek to find an easy way when you do something.
    If everything is easy you come to be careless.
    That's why the Great Sage says you should regard difficulty as a good teacher.

6. You shouldn't seek to benefit from your friends.
    If you do you will lose them.
    That's why the Great Sage says you should be sincere in keeping your friendships.

7. You shouldn't seek to win respect from others.
    If you do you come to be arrogant.
    That's why the Great Sage says you should make friends who are likely to criticize you.

8. You shouldn't seek to get merits from doing good deeds.
    If you do you always have the intention to do something.

That's why the Great Sage says you shouldn't pay much attention to it.

9. You shouldn't seek to make too much profit.

If you do you become ignorant.

That's why the Great Sage says you should be satisfied with little profits.

10. You shouldn't want to clear your name when you are upset at being mistreated.

If you do you come to cherish a grudge.

That's why the Great Sage says you should consider how being mistreated can really help your practice.

4. Song of Practice by Kyeong-Heo Sunim

All of a sudden, I think everying seems to be in a dream. All historical heroes and great warriors are resting in their graves on the Northern Mountain. Regardless of riches or honors, you must cross the river between life and death. Ah-ha, my flesh is like a dewdrop hanging over a leaf, like a candle in the wind.

Buddha, the teacher of the entire universe, clearly said "Enlighten, and become the awakened one, Buddha, and therefore end the vicious cycle of life and death, in the land where nothing is ever born nor destroyed, achieve the ultimate path of everlasting joyfulness. Each individual is expected to practice this way, and thus all eight thousand sutras were handed down generation by genera tion."

If you don't practice as a human being, it will be very difficult to get the chance to practice again; thus let us practice. When we speak of practicing, there are many ways to do it. Let me select and write them down in brief. Sitting, standing, watching, listening, wearing clothing, eating and talking with people, at every place and every moment, who is it that clearly perceives all of these thing?

My flesh is just a corpse, and all agonies are inherently empty. My inherent Buddha is able to see, hear, sit, rest, sleep, walk and travel around for ten thousand miles in the blink of an eye. My inherent mind has wondrous powers and is clearly connected to everything. What does it look like?

You should think about this question deeply, like a cat hunts for a rat, a starving person looks for food, a thirsty person for water, and a 60 or 70 year-old widow misses her children desperately after losing them. Do not forget these questions even for a single thought-moment, and rigorously search for the answers, so that you feel as if one thought- moment is like ten thousand years have passed. When thus you start to forget eating and sleeping, then you are close to enlightenment!

Once you get enlightenment, that is your original face of Buddha, sublime and mysterious, that is Amitahba and Shakyamuni Buddha, not young, not old, neither huge nor small, the utmost bliss and illumination of the world, and the eternal bliss of Nirvana, where there is no wheel of birth and death, where there is neither heaven nor hell, which never had any beginning.

At that time, you should visit a great master, receive recognition, cut off all doubts, and leave all attachments behind, and then live like an empty vessel according to one's causal conditions, liberate sentient beings you come to meet so that you can repay the favor you owe the Buddha.

If you keep the precepts, you will be born in the pure land of bliss. You should also make a great vow to learn the teachings of Buddha, you should look after ailing neighbors with great compassion, you should regard the empty bag of your body as if it was foam on a river.

Observing the favoring or unfavoring realms in a dream you should not get lazy, truly seeing my hollow mind as empty space, in every realms of the eight kinds of wind and the five desires, let's use this motionless mind like a great mountain. How can you study if you spend all your time talking nonsense without realizing your hair growing ever grayer. It is too late to lament when in pain on your deathbed.

Like limbs are chopped out and skull is broken, when organs and intestines are burning, you will become blind. Have you ever imagined your life in such a miserable state? Oh I'm so poor in that hell and that animal world! There is no way to be born a human while wandering along the path in the endless wheel of life.

The sages who kept their vows of ardent practice are now able to take leave of this mundane world whether standing or sitting, and they are able either to live, abide, or die at their own will. They are also able to exercise infinite manners of supernatural powers. Shall we not then practice with all our heart with a single pointed mind?

Death never waits for us, and every step could be our death step, like the steps of the cow that is being led to the slaughter house. The ancients never wasted time in practice. But how sluggish we are! The ancients even punctured their thighs with sharp points to stave off sleep. But how sluggish we are! The ancients stretched their legs and cried when their practice was forced to halt at the end of the day. But how sluggish we are!

We are leading drunken lives of retribution and ignorance. Alas, what a pitiful life it is! We are deaf to admonitions of good will. And heedless to reprimand. How could anyone straighten such careless and deluded minds, leading them along the right path?

It is foolish to be grasping and angry, foolish to fail into delusion and discriminate between things. There is no one to blame but oneself. The poor butterfly is flying headlong into the fire, not knowing that it is its own death. The mere observation of precepts and good conduct has no merit if one does not cultivate the mind. What a pity it is!

Read this admonition over and over again, day and night, and study hard without negligence and with little sleep. Lay this song open on the desk with great devotion. And reprove oneself every now and then.

All the waters of all the seas would be exhausted if I were to write all that I wanted to say. Although I am concluding my song, Everyone should bear in mind what I have warned. I still have more to say, But I will tell you when a stone totem pole bears a child.

THE GATELESS GATE

Preface

'Gateless gate' means there is a gate that there is no gate, and this gateless gate is the gate we must pass through.

Although the world seems to change quickly and move busily, nothing has changed in its essence. 10 years ago, 100 years ago, or 2600 years ago at the time of the Buddha …, likewise, the essential aspect has not changed.

There is a fish called swellfish. When swellfishes get caught on a fishing line and come out of the water, they greatly inflate their abdomen. It is said the self-defense system swellfish takes. But the same goes for people.

People who are aware of the extinction of death take a similar method with swellfish to overcome this problem. It is that people also take a method of self-extension, self-expansion. Living with the goal of success is one of those ways of self-extension and self-expansion. When these distortional thoughts are grouped together, they form a kind of culture, and the future generations will follow the flow of their surroundings before they even make their own judgements about these and other things. It is not my judgement or choice, but that I follow the method people around me do. The case of 'Jesus and Barabbas' is an example. As people shout Barabbas around them, so they shout out Barabbas after the people around them. What is my true judgement?

If you pass through this 'Gateless Gate', you will gain Right-eye and will no longer be rolled by the world, but will become the light of the world as a human being of great freedom.

Table of Contents

1. Jo Ju's Dog

A monk asked Seon Master Jo Ju, "Does a dog also have Buddha-nature or not?"

Jo Ju answered, "No(It doesn't have)."

Mu Mun's comment: For the practice of Seon you must pass through the gate of the patriarchs. To attain to marvelous enlightenment, you must completely extinguish all thoughts of the ordinary mind. If you do not pass the gate of the patriarchs or if your thinking road is not cut off, then you are a phantom haunting the weeds and trees. Now just tell me, What is the gate of a patriarch? Merely this one word, "No", is the one gate of Seon sect.

So it has come to be called "the Gateless Gate of the Seon sect." If you pass through it you will see Jo Ju face to face. Not only that, but you will walk hand in hand with the patriarchs, and it will be like your eyes and eyebrows merge with each other. You will see with the same eyes and hear with the same ears. Wouldn't it be a joyous and wonderful event! Wouldn't you like to pass through this gate? Is this not a pleasant thing to do?

If you want to pass this gate, you must work through every 365 bones in your body, through every 84,000 pores of your skin, filled with a solid lump of doubt of this question: What is "No"? and carry it day and night. However, do not think of this "No" as empty, or in relative terms of "has" or "has not". It would be just as if you had swallowed a red-hot iron ball that you can't vomit, no matter how hard you try. You have to extinguish all delusive thoughts and beliefs which you have cherished up to the present, and if you continue to practice for a very long time, then inside and outside will naturally become one. You alone will understand this by yourself like a mute has had a dream.

Then all of sudden, when you break through this Hwadu(No) it will astonish the heaven and shake the earth. It will be just as if you had snatched the great sword from General Gwan Wu: If you meet a Buddha, you will kill him. if you meet a patriarch, you will kill him. Though you may stand on the brink of life and death, attaining great freedom, you enjoy the bliss of Samadhi in the six realms and the four modes of birth.

So now, how will you have to practice? Using every bit of energy in your life, investigate this Hwadu "No" tightly. If your great doubt never cease, your Dharma lamp will suddenly become lit as if a candle in front of the alter is lighted by one touch of fire.

Verse

Dog and Buddha-nature
Buddhadharma have revealed fully
If there is a little "has" or "has not"
Your life would be lost!

2. Baek Jang and the Fox

Whenever Seon Master Baek Jang gave a Dharma talk, an old man was always there listening with the monks. At the end of each talk when the monks left so did he. But one day he remained after they had gone, and Baek Jang asked him, "Who are you?"

The old man replied, "I am not a human being, but I was a human being when the Mahakasyapa Buddha preached in this world. I was a Seon master and lived on this mountain. At that time one of my students asked me whether or not the enlightened man is subject to the law of cause and effect. I answered him, 'The enlightened man is not subject to the law of cause and effect.' For this answer, I received a fox's body for five hundred lifetimes, and I am still a fox. Now, I beg you, Master, please say a turning word on my behalf and release from the body of a fox." Whereupon he asked, "Does a perfectly enlightened person is subject to the law of cause and effect or not?"

Master said "The enlightened man doesn't ignore cause and effect."

Upon hearing this, the old man immediately became deeply enlightened. Paying homage with a deep bow, he said, "I am now liberated from this fox's form, but my corpse still remains behind this mountain. Please perform my funeral as a deceased monk." Then he disappeared.

The Seon Master had YuNa(chair monk in Seon monastery) strike the Mok-tak with a gavel and announce to the monks that after the meal there would be a funeral service for a deceased monk.

"No one was sick in the infirmary," wondered the monks. "What does our teacher mean?"

After dinner the Master led the monks to the foot of a rock behind the mountain and with his staff he poked out the dead body of a fox and then performed the ceremony of cremation.

That evening the Seon Master ascended the rostrum in the hall and told the monks the story.

Hwang Byeok, upon hearing the story, asked the Master, "The man of old gave the wrong answer and became a fox for five hundred lifetimes. But what would have happened if he had spoken correctly?"

The Seon Master said "You come here near me

and I will tell you." Hwang Byeok went near the Seon Master and slapped the teacher's face with his hand, the Seon Master clapped his hands and, laughing aloud, said, "I thought I would say the barbarian's beard was red, but here is a barbarian with a red beard!."

Mu Mun's comment: "The enlightened man is not subjected to." How can this answer make the monk a fox?

"The enlightened man doesn't ignore cause and effect." How can this answer make the fox emancipated?

If in regard to this you have the one eye, then you will understand that the former Back Jang enjoyed 500 lifetimes of grace fully as a fox.

Verse

Not being subjected to and not ignoring,
Two sides of one dice.
Not ignoring and not being subjected to,
A thousands mistakes, ten thousands mistakes.

3. Gu Ji's Finger

Gu Ji raised his finger whenever he was asked a question about Seon. He had a boy attendant whom a visitors asked, "what kind of teaching does your Master give?" The boy held up one finger too.

Gu Ji heard about this, he cut off the boy's finger with a knife. As the boy ran away, screaming with pain, Gu Ji called to him. When the boy turned his head to Gu Ji, Gu Ji raised up one finger. In that instant the boy was enlightened.

When Gu Ji was about to pass from this world he said to the assembled monks, "After I received this 'one-finger Seon' from Seon Master Cheon Ryong, I've used it all my life but I have not still exhausted it." Then he passed away.

Mu Mun's comment: The enlightenment, which Gu Ji and the boy attained, has nothing to do with a finger. If you understand this point, then Cheon Ryong, Gu Ji, the boy and yourself are all pierced with one skewer.

Verse

Gu Ji treats Cheon Ryong as a fool

And tested the boy with a sharp knife

Just like when the mountain deity (is called GeoLyeong) lifted his hand

And split the great mountain in half without effort.

4. The Barbarian Has No Beard

Master Hok Am said, "Why has the western barbarian(Bodhidharma) no beard?

Mu Mun's comment: If you practice Seon, you must actually practice it. If you become enlightened, it must be the real experience of enlightenment. You have to meet this barbarian once face-to-face. But if you say you met him, it already becomes two.

Verse:

Do not talk about dreams
In front of a fool.
The word that the barbarian has no beard
Obscures the bright and obvious.

5. Hyang Eom Mounts the Tree

Master Hyang Eom said, "When you mount on a tree and bite a branch with your mouth without touching the tree with your hands or stepping on the tree with your feet, let's suppose there is someone under the tree and he asks 'the meaning of Bodhidharma's coming from the west', at that time if you don't answer, it goes against what he asked, and if you answer, you will lose your life. At such a time, how should you answer?"

Mu Mun's comment: Even if your eloquence flows like a river, it is of no use. Even if you can expound all of the sutras, it is still of no avail. If you can answer correctly, you will give life to those who have been dead, and put to death to those who have been alive. Otherwise you must wait for a day in the distant future and ask Maitreya Buddha.

Verse

Master Hyang Eom is really absurd,
His scathing remarks have no end.

He stops the mouths of the monks
And makes ghost eyes rise all over the body.

6. Buddha Holds Up a Flower

Once in ancient times, When the Buddha gave a Dharma talk for the assembly on Vulture Peak, he held up a single flower and showed it to the community. Every one was silent, only Mahakasyapa smiled at this revelation.

At that time Buddha said, "I have the treasury of the true Dharma eye, the mystical mind of Nirvana, the true form of no-form, the subtle gate of the Dharma. It does not depend on letters, being specially transmitted outside all teachings. Now I entrust Mahakasyapa with this."

Mu Mun's comment: Golden-faced Gautama insolently suppressed noble people and made them lowly. He sells dog meat under the sign of ram's head. It could be said it was praiseworthy. However, What if all the audience at that time had laughed together? How could he have transmitted the true Dharma eye? And again, if Mahakasyapa had not smiled, how could he have transmitted it? If you says that the true Dharma eye can be transmitted, then it is for the golden-face old man to cheat country people. If you say it cannot be transmitted, why was it allowed to only one Mahakasyapa?

Verse

> When holding up a flower,
> The tail was already revealed.
> Mahakasyapa smiled,
> Nobody on earth or in heaven knows what to do.

7. Jo Ju's "Wash the Bowl"

A monk asked Seon Master Jo Ju, "I have just entered this monastery. Please give me instructions, great master."

Jo Ju asked him, "Have you eaten your rice gruel?"

The monk answered, "I have eaten."

Jo Ju said, "Then wash your bowl."

At that moment the monk attained some realization.

Mu Mun's comment: Jo Ju, opening his mouth, showed his gall bladder and revealed his heart and liver. If the monk, hearing it, did not really grasp the fact, he would mistake a bell for a pot.

Verse

Since it is too clear
Rather, it is slow to get.
If you early acknowledge that the candlelight is fire,
It's been a long time since rice was cooked.

8. Hae Jung makes a Cart

Seon Master Wol Am asked a monk, "Hae Jung made a cart with one-hundred spokes, but he took off both wheels and removed the axle, what would he make clear about the cart?"

Mu Mun's comment: If you realize this at once, your eye will be like a shooting star and your spiritual activity will be like a flash of light.

Verse

At the point where the wheels spin,
Even an accomplished person is confused.
It is four directions, above and below,
And South, north, east and west

9. The Buddha of Supreme Penetration and Superior Wisdom

A monk asked Seon Master Cheong Yang of Heung Yang, "The Buddha of Supreme Penetration and Superior Wisdom sat in the meditation hall for ten kalpas, but the Dharma of the Buddha did not manifest itself and he could not attain Buddhahood. What is the meaning of this?"

Seon Master Cheong Yang said, "Your question is reasonable indeed."

The monk asked again, "He already sat in monastery but why did he not attain Buddhahood?"

Seon Master Cheong Yang said, "Because he does not become Buddha."

Mu Mun's comment: I will allow his realization, but I will not admit his understanding. When even an ordinary person attains realization he is a saint. Though one is a saint, if he understands with distinctions, he is just an ordinary person.

Verse

Realizing mind and gaining peace cannot be compared to cultivating body.

If the mind is realized, they don't worry about the body.

If both body and mind are completely realized,

A holy hermit does not wish to be appointed lord.

10. Cheong Se's Loneliness and Poverty

A monk named Cheong Se asked of Jo San, "Cheong Se is alone and poor. I beg you, Master, please help me to become prosperous."

Seon Master Jo San called out "Cheong Se."

Cheong Se responded, "Yes, Master."

Seon Master Jo San said, "Even though you have already drunk three cups of the finest wine and still you say that you have not yet moistened your lips."

Mu Mun's comment: What is the true intention of Cheong Se's unskillful behavior? Jo San has the penetrating eye and thoroughly discerns the monk's capacity. But though that may have been the case, just tell me, at what point Cheong Se drink the wine?

Verse

Honest poverty like Beom Dan(a famous scholar's name)

Spirit like Hang Wu(a famous soldier name)

Without a single penny for his livelihood
They dare to compete with each other for wealth.

11. Jo Ju Examines the Hermits

Seon Master Jo Ju went to a hermitage and asked, "Is there?, is there?"

The hermit raised his fist.

Seon Master Jo Ju said, "The water is too shallow for a ship to anchor." And he left.

Seon Master Jo Ju went again to another hermitage and asked, "Is there?, is there?"

The hermit also raised his fist.

Seon Master Jo Ju said "Freely you give, freely you take away, freely you kill, freely you give life." And immediately bowed.

Mu Mun's comment: Each hermit raised his fist the same way. But Why is one accepted and the other rejected? Where is the fault?

If on this point you say a turning word, then you can see that Seon Master Jo Ju's tongue has no bone so he both helps others stand up and knocks them over as he pleases. Though that is the case, could it rather be true that Seon Master Jo Ju was tested by the two hermits? If you say that there is a distinction of superiority and inferiority between the two hermits, you have not yet the eye of realization. On the other hand, if you say there is no difference between the two hermits, then you also have no eye of realization.

Verse

> An eye like a shooting star,
> A response like lightning.
> Both a sword that kills,
> And a sword that gives life.

12. Seo Am Calls Himself "Master"

Every day Seon Master Seo Am used to call to himself, "Master!" and then answer, "Yes!" And after that he would add, "Stay awake!" and then he answer "Yes! Yes!" "Don't be deceived by others afterwards." "No! No!"

Mu Mun's comment: Old Seo Am both buys and sells out himself. Palyfully he shows the faces of many ghosts and goblins. But why does he do that? Look! One is calling, one is answering, one is keeping awake and one is saying not to be deceived by others. If you acknowledge anything of them, it is still not correct. If you imitate Seon Master Seo Am, it would be the understanding of a fox.

Verse

The reason those who learn the Way don't realize the truth
Is because they perceive the manifestations of consciousness as the self from before.
It is the root of birth and death from countless

past;

    Fools take it for the original-self.

13. Deok Sahn Carries His Bowl

One day Seon Master Deok Sahn went to the dining room, carrying his bowl. Ven. Seol Bong asked him "Old Master, the bell has not yet rung nor the drum sounded. where are you going with your bowls?" Deok Sahn immidiately went back to his room.

Seol Bong told to Ven. Am Du about this. Am Du said, "Great Deok Sahn though he is, he has not realized the last word." Hearing of this, Master Deok Sahn asked his attendant to call Am Du to him.

"Don't you approve of me?"

Ven. Am Du secretly whispered his intention so Master Deok Sahn stopped talking and said nothing. The next day when Master Deok Sahn ascended the rostrum, his talk was quite different from usual.

Ven. Am Du went to the front of the hall, clapped his hands, and laughed loudly, saying, "Wonderful! our old master has realized the last word. From now on, he will not be subjected to anyone on earth."

Mu Mun's comment: As for the last word, neither Am Du nor Deok Sahn have even seen it in a dream. When I checked it closely, it is just like puppets on a shelf.

Verse

> If you grasp the first word
> Then you also realize the last word.
> But both the last word and the first word
> Are not this one word.

14. Nam Jeon Cuts the Cat in Two

Seon Master Nam Jeon saw that the monks of the eastern and western halls was arguing over a cat. The Master seized the cat and told the monks, "If any of you say a word, I will spare the cat. If you can't, I will kill it right now!" But no one answered, Master Nam Jeon finally cut the cat in two pieces.

That evening, Ven. Jo Ju returned and Master Nam Jeon told him about the day's events. Thereupon Jo Ju took off his sandals, put them on his head, and walked out. Nam Jeon then said, "If you had been there, you could have saved the cat."

Mu Mun's comment: Now, tell me! Why did Jo Ju put his sandals on his head? If anyone answers this question, he(she) will understand exactly how Master Nam Jeon enforced the edict. If not, then he(she) is in danger!

Verse

If Ven. Jo Ju had been there

He would have done the opposite;

If Ven. Jo Ju snatched away the knife,

Then even Seon Master Nam Jeon would have begged for his life.

15. Dong Sahn's Three Rounds of Blows

Ven. Dong Sahn came to Seon Master Un Mun for instruction. Master Un Mun asked him, "where have you come from recently?"

Dong Sahn said, "I came from Sa Do village."

Master Un Mun asked, "Where were you during the summer retreat?"

Dong Sahn replied, "I was at the temple Boja-sa, south of the lake."

Master Un Mun asked, "When did you leave there?"

Dong Sahn said, "On the twenty-fifth of August."

Master Un Mun said, "I should give you three rounds of blows with a staff, but today I forgive you."

The next day Dong Sahn bowed to Un Mun and asked, "Yesterday you forgave me three blows but I don't know where was I at fault?"

Master Un Mun said, "Oh, you rice bag! Have you been wandering about like that, now west of the river, now south of the lake?"

Ven. Dong Sahn was greatly enlightened by these words.

Mu Mun's comment: At that time, Master Un Mun had given Dong Sahn the essential food of Seon and awakened him to an active Seon spirit, his Seon family gate would not have become so desolate. Dong Sahn struggled with himself all night long in the sea of good and bad and at daybreak came to Master Un Mun again, Master Un Mun gave him a further push to break through. Althought Dong Sahn attained enlightenment at that point, he still could not be called bright.

Now I ask you, "Should Dong Sahn have received three rounds of blows or not?" If you say yes, then you are saying that all the grasses, trees, and everything also deserve to be beaten; if you say no, then Master Un Mun was just speaking nonsense. If you clearly grasp this, you are breathing through one mouth with Dong Sahn.

Verse

The lioness has a puzzling way of teaching its cubs;
As soon as the cub hesitates to jump forward, she quickly flips the cub over and drop it.

Unexpectedly, Master Un Mun gave a checkmate again,

The first arrow was barely struck, but the second one was pierced deeply.

16. The Bell and the Seven-Stripes Robe

Seon Master Un Mun said, "The world is vast and wide like this, why do you put on your seven-stripes robe at the sound of the bell?"

Mu Mun's comment: Generally speaking, in practicing and studying Seon, it is most detestable to follow sounds and pursue colors. Even though you may become enlightened through hearing sounds and come to realize mind by seeing colors, this is not something special. People don't know that Seon monks, riding on sounds and controling colors, see everything clearly, and are free to control things one by one. Though that may be true, please tell me, does sound come to the ear, or does the ear go to the sound?

Even though you have extinguished both sound and silence, how could you say at this point? If you hear with the ears, it may be difficult to comprehend, but if you hear with your eyes, for the first time it will become intimate.

Verse

With realization, all things are of one family;

Without realization, everything is separate and different;

Even without realization, all things are of one family;

With realization, immediately everything is separate and different.

17. The National Teacher Calls Three Times

The National Teacher Hye Chung called his attendant three times, and three times his attendant responded. The National Teacher then said, "I had thought that I was betraying you, but rather it was you who was betraying me."

Mu Mun's comment: The National Teacher called his attendant three times and his tongue dropped to the ground. The attendant responded three times, revealed himself with light.

The National Teacher was old and lonely? he pushed down the cow's head and forced it to eat grass. But the attendant would have none of it; delicious food has little attraction for a man who has had enough to eat.

Now, tell me! Which is where they betray each other? When the country is prosperous, talented people are esteemed; when the home is wealthy, the child's manners worsen.

Verse

Putting an iron yoke with no holes on the people,

This mistake affects one's descendants and can not be neglected.

If you want to support the gate of Seon and sustain the house of Seon,

You must climb the sword mountain with bare feet.

18. Dong Sahn's Three Pounds of Flax

A monk asked Seon Master Dong Sahn, "What is Buddha?" Dong Sahn said, "Three pounds of flax."

Mu Mun's comment: Old monk Dong Sahn got the clam-shell Seon. Slightly opening the two halves of the shell, he exposed his liver and intestines. Though that is the case, tell me, where do you see Dong Sahn?

Verse

The 'Three pounds of flax' that suddenly said;
The words are intimate and the meaning is even more intimate.
A person who comes and speaks about right and wrong
Is a person who get caught by right and wrong.

19. Ordinary Mind Is the Way

Ven. Jo Ju asked Seon Master Nam Jeon, "What is the Way?"

Master Nam Jeon said, "Ordinary mind is the Way."

Jo Ju asked again, "Should I direct myself toward it or not?"

Nam Jeon said, "If you try to turn toward it, you go against it."

Jo Ju asked again, "If I do not try to turn toward it, how can I know that it is the way?"

Nam Jeon said, "The Way does not belong to knowing or not-knowing. Knowing is delusion; not-knowing is a blank consciousness. If you truly become master of the Way beyond all doubt, it is clearly vast and boundless like empty space. How can it be talked about on a level of right and wrong?" At these words, Jo Ju suddenly attained enlightenment.

Mu Mun's comment: Seon Master Nam Jeon was asked by Jo Ju, and then Master Nam Jeon's base was like the roof tile was shattered and ice melted, he could not excuse. Even though Jo Ju had come to realization, he had to cultivate for another thiry years in order to finally realize it.

Verse

> The flowering spring, autumn's moon
> The summer's cool breezes, the winter's snow;
> If useless things do not hang in your mind,
> This is a good season in the human world.

20. A Person of Great Strength

Seon Master Song Won said, "Why is it that a person of great strength can't lift his(her) own leg and stand up?" He also said, "It is not with the tongue that we speak."

Mu Mun's comment: Seon Master Song Won poured out all that he had in his intestines and belly. But there is nobody who can recognize this. Even if there is someone who realizes this immediately, he(she) will have to come to me and be severely beaten with my staff. Why is that? If you want to know whether it is pure gold or not, you have to test it in fire.

Verse

Lifting a leg, I knock over the Fragrant Ocean;
Lowering my head, I look down on the four dhyana heavens.
This single body can't be placed anywhere.
Hopefully, please add a word to this poem.

21. Un Mun's A Dried Shit Stick

A monk asked Seon Master Un Mun "What is Buddha?"

The Master Un Mun said, "A dried shit stick."

Mu Mun's comment: Master Un Mun's household was poor, so it was difficult for him to prepare simple food; he was so busy that he didn't even have a chance to scribble something down. Any old how, he took up the dried shit stick to support Seon school; thus it is easy to guess how the rise and fall of Buddha-Dharma will be.

Verse

Lightning flashes,
Flint sparks
A moment's blinking —
It's already missed.

22. Mahakasyapa's Flagpole

Ananda asked Mahakasyapa, "Aside from the golden robe, What else did the World-Honoured One transmit to you?"

Mahakasyapa called, "Ananda!"

Ananda answered, "Yes, Master."

Mahakasyapa said, "Knock down the flagpole in front of gate."

Mu Mun's comment: If you can give a suitable word here, you will soon see that the Dharma assembly at Vulture Peak has not finished and still continues today. If not, even if you have keeping something in mind from the days of Vipashyin(the first Buddha among the seven past Buddhas) until now, you still can not attain the mystical realm of enlightenment.

Verse

Why isn't the question as kind as the answer?

How many people can have glaring eyes at this point!

Elder brother calls, younger brother answers -
the family shame is revealed.

This is another spring that has nothing to do
with yin and yang.

23. Do Not Think of Good and Bad

The sixth patriarch was once pursued by the Ven. Hye Myong as far as Mount Daeyu. The sixth patriarch saw Hye Myong pursuing him, so he put his robe and bowl on the rock and said, "This robe represents the faith in the Dharma, how can it be competed for by force? If you desire to take them, take them now."

Hye Myong tried to pick it up, but it was as immovable as a mountain. Terrified and trembling with awe, he said, "I came for the Dharma, not the robe. I beg you, please give me your teaching!"

The sixth patriarch said, "Do not think of good and bad. At that very moment, what is your original face?"

At that instant, Hye Myong suddenly attained great enlightenment, and his whole body was covered with sweat, and as tears poured down his face he bowed and asked, "Besides the secret words and secret meaning, is there any another teaching?" The sixth patriarch said, "What I have just told to you is not a secret at all. If you reflect on your own original face, the secret will be inside of you."

Hye Myong said, "Though I practiced with the other monks on Hwang Mae Mountain, I have never realized what my original face is. Now, thanks to your instruction, I know it is like a man who drinks water and knows for himself whether it is cold or warm. Now, you are my teacher."

The sixth patriarch said, "If you think like that, then let's both have Hwang Mae for our teacher. Be careful to maintain what you have realized."

Mu Mun's comment: It should be said of the sixth patriarch that his action sprang from urgent circumstance and he had a lot of concern. It is as if he peels a fresh lychee, takes out the seeds, and put it in your mouth, so that all you have to do is to swallow it once.

Verse

It can't be described! It can't be pictured!
It can't be sufficiently praised! Stop trying to grasp it with your head!
The original face has nowhere to hide;
Even When the world is destroyed, it is inde-

structible.

24. Leaving Speech and Silence

A monk asked Seon Master Pung Hyeol, "Whether speaking or keeping silence, one is either caught by the fault of transcendence or subtle functionality; How can we work without transgressions?"

Seon Master Pung Hyeol said, "I always remember March in Gang Nam, as there are hundreds of fragrant flowers where the patridges sing."

Mu Mun's comment: Seon Master Pung Hyeol's spirit is like lightening, so that he gains the road and immediately walks along. But why does he sit on the tip of the ancient one's tongue and not cut it off?

If you realize exactly at this point, you can find the way beyond all hindrances by yourself. Just leaving the world of all languages, give me one word!

Verse

Without using a dignified phrase,
Before speaking, it is already manifested.

If you go chattering glibly
Know that you are making a big mistake.

25. The Sermon of the Third Seat

In a dream Seon Master Ang Sahn went to Maitreya's place and sat in the third seat. A Ven. monk then struck the gavel and said, "Today the third seat is due to give the Dharma speech."

Seon Master Ang Sahn stood up, struck the gavel, and said, "The Dharma of Mahayana is beyond the four propositions and severs the hundred negations. Listen carefully, listen carefully!"

Mu Mun's comment: Tell me! Did he preach or did he not? If you open your mouth, you are lost. If you shut your mouth, you lose your life. Even if you neither open nor shut your mouth, it is a hundred and eight thousand miles away.

Verse

Sunlight shining brightly in the blue sky
He speaks of a dream in a dream.
How bizarre and strange ...
He deceives the whole assemble.

26. Two Monks Roll Up the Blinds

Seon Master Beop An of the monastery Cheong Ryang Won was asked for instruction by some monks before the midday meal. The Master pointed to the blinds. At that moment, two monks stood up together and rolled up the blinds.

Seon Master Beop An said, "One has gained, the other has lost."

Mu Mun's comment: Now, tell me! Which one has gained and which one has lost? If you have the correct Dharma eye at this point, you will know where National teacher Cheong Ryang was mistaken. But even so, you should not make distinctions about gaining and losing.

Verse

The blind being rolled, bright clarity penetrates the great empty space.

But even the great empty space does not match up to my school's the fundamental meaning.

Even so,

How can compare with that throw away the great empty space and even slightest wind can't pass through?

27. Not Mind, Not Buddha

A monk asked Seon Master Nam Jeon, "Is there any Dharma that has not been preached to people ?"

Nam Jeon said, "There is."

The monk asked "What is the Dharma which has never been preached to people?"

Nam Jeon said, "It is not mind; it is not Buddha; it is not a thing."

Mu Mun's comment: Nam Jeon was merely asked this one question, and he used up all his possessions. He must have been greatly upset.

Verse

Excessive kindness damages virtue.

No-words is indeed the true virtue.

Even though the blue sea changes into a mulbelly field,

I will never speak to you.

28. Yong Dam's Name Echoed Long

The Ven. Deok Sahn kept asking for instruction until at night. Seon Master Yong Dam said, "The night is late, Why don't you retire?" So Deok Sahn bowed and opened the blinds, and went out the door. Observing it is very dark outside, Deok Sahn turned back and said, "It's pitch black outside."

Seon Master Yong Dam offered Deok Sahn a lighted candle to find his way. Just as Deok Sahn received it, Seon Master Yong Dam blew it out. At that moment the mind of Deok Sahn was opened and made a deep bow.

Seon Master Yong Dam asked, "What have you realized?" Deok Sahn said, "From now on, I will never doubt the words of all old masters."

The next day Seon Master Yong Dam ascended the rostrum and said, "There is a man here whose teeth are like a forest of swords, and whose mouth is like a blood bowl. Though you hit him hard with this staff, he will not even turn his head back. Someday he will mount the highest peak and carry my teaching there."

Deok Sahn brought all his Sutra commentaries

and notes in front of the Buddha hall, held up a torch and said, "Though you have mastered all abstruse teachings, it is like putting a single hair in the great sky. Even if you have completely expounded all the truths of the world, it is like a drop of water thrown into a big ravine." He then burned all his commentaries and notes, bowed to his teacher, and left.

Mu Mun's comment: Before Ven. Deok Sahn had crossed the border, his mind was full of resentment and his mouth speechless with anger. He wanted to eradicate the teachings of those who advocated a special transmission outside of the scriptures, so he proudly came to the south. When he got to the land of Yae Ju, he asked an old woman if he could buy a lunch from her. The old woman said, "Venerable, what kind of books are inside your sack?"

Deok Sahn said, "Those are commentarries on the Diamond Sutra."

The old woman said, "In that sutra, it says 'The past mind cannot be held, the present mind cannot be held, the future mind cannot be held.'

Venerable monk, with which mind would you have your lunch?"

When Deok Sahn heard this question, he became stuck and he couldn't say anything. But he didn't completely die away, and he asked her, "Is there a Seon Master near here?" The old woman said, "Seon Master Yong Dam lives about five miles from here."

After Deok Shan arrived where Seon Master Yong Dam was, he was entirely defeated. It was quite different from when he had started his journey. Yong Dam was like a parent who has lost all sense of shame because their child is so cute; seeing a live ember in Deok Sahn, he immediately threw muddy water over his head to extinguish it. Looking at this coolly, it is a scene of a farce.

Verse

> Seeing the face is better than hearing the name;
> Hearing the name is better than seeing the face.
> Even though he saved nostril
> Alas, he lost his eyes!

29. Not the Wind, Not the Flag

Two monks saw a flag fluttering in the wind and began to argue with each other. One said, "The flag is moving."

The other said, "The wind is moving." They argued back and forth, and they didn't make sense.

The sixth patriarch said, "It is not the wind that moves. It is not the flag that moves. It is your mind that moves." The two monks were awe-struck by this.

Mu Mun's comment: It is not the wind that moves; It is not the flag that moves; It is not the mind that moves. Where can you see the patriarch? If you clearly grasp it, you will understand that the two monks bought iron but ended up getting gold, and the patriarch impatiently exposed a scene of mistake.

Verse

The wind moves, the flag moves, the mind moves;
These words must be punished with a warrant.

They only knew how to open their mouths,
But they didn't know that they fell into the words.

30. This Mind Is Buddha

Ven. Dae Mae asked Seon Master Ma Jo, "What is Buddha?"

Seon Master Ma Jo said, "This mind is Buddha."

Mu Mun's comment: If you can directly grasp this phrase, then you wear the Buddha's clothes, eat the Buddha's food, speak the Buddha's words, and do Buddha's deeds; you are Buddha himself. Even so, Dae Mae led not a few people into misreading the scale on the balance. How could he know that even mentioning Buddha should make a man(woman) rinse his(her) mouth for three days! If such a person hears the phrase "This mind is Buddha", he will cover his ears and run away.

Verse

The blue sky, brightly shining sun,
Never search for!
If you ask 'what is it' again,
It is like you shout innocence while holding the stolen goods.

31. Seon Master Jo Ju Sees Through an Old Woman

A monk asked an old woman, "Which way to Oh Dae Mountain?"

The old woman said, "Only go straight." When the monk proceeded a few steps, she said to herself, "This good monk also goes that way." Later someone told this incident to Seon Master Jo Ju.

Seon Master said, "Wait, I will go and see through the old woman for you."

The next day, Seon Master went and asked the same question, and the old woman gave the same answer.

Seon Master returned and told the community, "I have seen through the old woman of Oh Dae Mountain for you."

Mu Mun's comment: The old woman just sat in her barracks and knew how to plan the strategy, but she did not know how spies sneak in behind her barracks. Old Jo Ju played the spy's work well that stealed the camp and deprived her of fortress, but he didn't have the air of a great man.

Pondering the matter, both had their faults. Now, tell me! At what point did Jo Ju investigate the old woman?

Verse

> The question is the same,
> The answer is also similar.
> There is sand in the rice,
> There is thorns in the mud.

32. A Non-Buddhist Asks Buddha

A Non-Buddhist asked the World-Honored One, "I don't ask about words, I don't ask about no-words."

The World-Honored One just sat still.

The non-Buddhist praised him and said, "The World-Honored One, with his great love and compassion, has opened the clouds of my delusion and enabled me to enter enlightenment." Then, bowing, he left.

Ananda asked the Buddha, "what did the non-Buddhist realize that made him praise you so much?" The World-Honored One replied, "It is as if a fine horse runs even at the shadow of a whip."

Mu Mun's comment: Even though Ananda was the disciple of the Buddha, his opinion did not surpass that of non-Buddhist. Now tell me, "How far is the distance between the non-Buddhist and Buddha's disciple?"

Verse

Walking on the edge of a sword,
Running on thin ice.
Without using steps or a ladder,
He releases his hand from the cliff.

33. No Mind, No Buddha

A monk asked Seon Master Ma Jo, "What is Buddha?"

Seon Master Ma Jo said, "No mind, No Buddha."

Mu Mun's comment: If you can understand this, your Seon practice is finished

Verse

If you meet a swordsman, you may present him your sword,

If you don't meet a poet, you should not offer him your poem.

When you meet others, say only three-quarters of it.

You should not donate everything.

34. Knowing Is Not the Way

Nam Jeon said, "Mind is not Buddha; Knowing is not the Way."

Mu Mun's comment: It should be said of Nam Jeon that he has now grown old and knows no shame. He opened his mouth for a moment and he exposed the disgrace of his own household. However, there are very few who appreciate his kindness.

Verse

When the sky is clear, the sun appears;
When the rain falls, earth is wet.
Though he preaches everything with all his heart,
It is just worried that the listeners won't believe it.

35. Cheon Nyeo's Soul Has Left

Seon Master Oh Jo asked a monk, "Cheon Nyeo's soul has left her, which one is the true Cheon Nyeo?"

Mu Mun's comment: If you realize the true one in this, you will know that getting out of one shell and entering another is just like a traveler staying at an motel. If it's not that case, don't wander dizzily looking outward.

When earth, water, fire, and air are suddenly scattered, you will be just like a crab which has fallen into boiling water, struggling with seven arms and eight legs. At that time, don't say I didn't warn you.

Verse

The clouds and the moon are the same;
Valleys and the mountains are all different.
Wonderful, what a wonderful!
Is this one or is this two?

※ Cheon Nyeo: 'Cheon Nyeo' is the name of a girl, this old story is as follow;

A man named Jang Gam lived in the chinese land of Hyeong Yang, and he had one beautiful daughter named Cheon Nang(= Cheon Nyeo), Jang Gam often used to promise his nephew Wang Ju that he could marry his daughter. However, a government official in the area was captivated by Cheon Nang's beauty and asked her to marry; Jang Gam forget about his previous commitment and sent her off to be married to him.

Wang Ju and Cheon Nang were broken-hearted, Wang Ju decided to leave that place in order to put her out of his mind, when he boarded a ship and was about to depart, suddenly Cheon Nang appeared and the two of them escaped together to the faraway land of Chok. They lived happily there for next five years and had a child.

During this time, one day Cheon Nang began to get sicker and sicker, and believing that this sick was made by the retribution for the pain that they had caused their parents, they headed home in order to formally ask their parents' permission for marriage. After arriving in the port near his hometown, Wang Ju left Cheon Nang in the boat and went to her father Jang Gam to explain what had happened all that while. But Jang Gam was very astonished and said that my daughter, Cheon Nang, for a long time, had been lying sick for in the woman's quarters. All of the family members ran to the women's quarters, while the story was being told, Cheon Nang had suddenly regained her strength. Jang Gam sent someone to the boat to bring Cheon Nang to his house.

At the moment when the other Cheon Nang came home by cart and the Cheon Nang who was walking out of the room met face to face in the yard, the two of them became one. When Jang Gam asked her how in the world this could have happened, Cheon Nang answered, "I couldn't bear to let my husband go alone, so it seems my soul followed him onto the ship." At this point, Jang Gam and his family realized what had happened. Cheon Nang had been constantly sick in the room, like someone in a daze, because her spirit had followed Wang Ji.

36. Meeting a Sage on the Road

Seon Master Oh Jo said, "If you meet a person on the road who has accomplished the Way, do not address the person with words or silence. Now, tell me! how will you address that person?"

Mu Mun's comment: In such a case, if you can answer this question properly, wouldn't it truly be joyous and gratifying? But if you cannot, you should look fot it attentively everywhere.

Verse

Meeting a person on the road who has accomplished the Way,
Do not address the person with words or silence.
When punching his cheek with fist,
If he knows right away, he is the person who really knows.

37. The Cypress Tree in Front of the Courtyard

A monk asked Seon Master Jo Ju, "What is the meaning of the patriarch's coming from the West?"

The Seon Master Jo Ju said, "The cypress tree in front of the courtyard."

Mu Mun's comment: If one sees Jo Ju's answer clearly, there is no Shakyamuni Buddha in the past, no Maitreya Buddha in the future

Verse

Words cannot describe everything.

The heart's message cannot be delivered in words.

If one follows words literally, he will be lost,

If one is stagnate within words, he will be deluded.

38. A Buffalo passes Through a Window

Ven. Oh Jo said, "(Enlightenment is) For example, it's just like a water buffalo passing through a latticed window; the head, horns, and four legs have all passed through (but the tail don't have passed through), Why can't the tail pass through?"

Mu Mun's comment: If anyone can open the single eye at this point and say a turning word, it is to repay the four kinds of kindness above and help the sentient beings in the three realms below. But if you can't do that, you should reflect again on the tail.

Verse

If it passes through, it will fall into the trench;
If it turns back, it will be destroyed.
This tiny little tail,
What a really bizarre thing it is!

39. Un Mun's "Fallen in Words"

A monk asked Seon Master Un Mun, "Bright light serenely illuminates the whole universe . . ."

Before he had even finished the first line, Master Un Mun suddenly interrupted, "Aren't those the words of Jang Jol Su Jae?"

The monk replied, "Yes, they are."

Master Un Mun said, "You have fallen in words."

Afterwards, Seon Master Sa Shim brought this story and said, "Tell me, at what point did that monk get fallen in words?"

Mu Mun's comment: At this point If you realize that Master Un Mun's outstanding activity and how the monk fell in the words, you are worthy to become a teacher of men and heavenly beings. If you are not yet clear about it, then you can't even save yourself.

Verse

Casting a fishing line in a swift stream,

Those who are greedy for bait are caught.
As soon as they open their mouth a bit
They lose their lives.

40. Kicking Over a Water Jug

When Ven. Wi San was under Seon Master Baek Jang's community, he had the position of kitchen master. Seon Master Baek Jang wished to choose leader of Dae Wi Mountain Sangha, so that he called the head monk and the rest of his disciples together to have them present their views and said that the exceptional person should be sent. Then he took a water jug, put it on the ground, and asked, "You may not call it a water jug. What will you all call it?"

The head monk said, "It can't be called a wooden shoe."

Seon Master Baek Jang then asked Ven. Wi San, whereupon Wi San kicked over the water jug and left.

Master Baek Jang burst out laughing and said, "The head monk has been defeated by a country bumpkin!" So he ordered Wi San to found the new monastery.

Mu Mun's comment: Although Wi San once took courage, alas, he couldn't jump out of Master

Baek Jang's trap. If we look at it closely, he favored the heavy and not the light. What was that reason? Look! He took off his headband, he put on an iron yoke.

Verse

Tossing away the strainer and wooden-ladle,

He is confidently bumped into and cut off hindrances at once.

Baek Jang's various barriers couldn't also stop him,

He pours out Buddha as many as flax from the tip of his feet.

41. Bodhidharma Pacifies the Mind

Bodhidharma sat facing the wall. The second patriarch, standing in the snow, cut off his arm and said, "Your disciple's mind is restless. I beg Master to settle it for me."

Bodhidharma said, "Bring me that mind, I will settle it for you."

The second patriarch said, "I have tried to find my mind but I cannot find it."

Bodhidharma said, "I have already settled it for you."

Mu Mun's comment: That broken-toothed old barbarain came thousands of miles over the sea deliberately; it is as if he raised waves where there was no wind. Later he got one disciple, a cripple who was not clear in his six senses. Ha! The fools do not even know the four letters of the alphabet.

Verse

Coming from the West, pointing directly to it;
This happened by the transmission.

The one who disturbs the monasteries
Is originally you.

42. A Woman Comes Out Of Samadhi

In the time of Buddha Shakyamuni, Manjusri went to the place where Buddhas were assembled and found that each Buddha had returned to his own Buddha-land; only one woman remained, sitting in samadhi close to Buddha.

Manjusri asked the Buddha, "Why can that woman sit near the Buddha while I can't?"

The Buddha said, "You should awaken that woman from samadhi and ask her yourself."

Manjusri walked around the woman three times and snapped his fingers, took her up to the Brahman heaven, and used all his miraculous powers, but he couldn't still awaken the woman from samadhi.

The World-honored One said, "Even a hundred or a thousand Manjusris would not be able to bring her from samadhi. Down below, past twelve hundred million lands as innumerable as the sand of the Ganges, is the first level Bodhisattva Mang Myong. He will be able to arouse her from her samadhi."

No sooner had the Buddha spoken than that Bodhisattva sprang up from the earth and bowed to the Buddha. The World-honored One asked him to awaken the woman from samadhi. The Bodhisattva Mang Myong went in front of the woman and snapped his fingers once, and in that instant the woman came out from her samadhi.

Mu Mun's comment: Old Shakyamuni set a country drama on stage but this coudn't accomplish even a trivial thing. Tell me! Manjusri was the teacher of seven Buddhas; why couldn't he bring the woman from samadhi? Mang Myong was a first level Bodhisattva; how could he arouse the woman from samadhi?

If you understand this intimately, surging delusive consciousness is nothing other than greatest samadhi.

Verse

Whether they can awaken her from samadhi or not,

Both have their own freedom.

One is wearing a ghost's head mask and the other is wearing a devil's face mask.

Even failure is a taste for the arts.

43. Su Sahn's Jukpi

Seon Master Su Sahn held up a Jukpi(bamboo clapper) and showed it to assembly and said, "All of you, if you call this a Jukpi, you are in conflict with its fact. If you do not call this a Jukpi, it is for you to make against the fact. Tell me! all of you, what will you call it?"

Mu Mun's comment: If you call this a Jukpi, you are in conflict with its fact. If you do not call this a Jukpi, it is for you to make against the fact. You must not speak, nor must not speak. Quickly tell me! Quickly tell me!

Verse

Holding up the Jukpi,
He conducted the order to kill and to give life.
Mixing 'making against' and 'conflict', and wielding it swiftly,
So even Buddhas and patriarchs beg for their lives.

44. Pa Cho's Staff

Seon Master Pa Cho said to the assembly, "If you have a staff, I will give a staff to you. If you have no staff, I will take it away from you."

Mu Mun's comment: Relying on this, I cross a river that has no bridge and, with it, return to the village on a moonless night. But if you call it a staff, you will enter hell like an arrow.

Verse

The depths and shallows everywhere
Are all within his grip!
Holding up heaven and supporting the earth,
Everywhere it resounds far and wide the spirit of our sect.

45. Who Is That Person?

Seon Master (Beop) Yeon of Dong-Sahn(Eastern Mountian) said, "Even Shakyamuni and Maitreya are servants of that person. Who is that person?"

Mu Mun's comment: If you clearly recognize that person, it's like encountering your own father at the crossroads, so there is no need to ask anyone whether it's your father or not.

Verse

    Do not draw another's bow,
    Do not ride another's horse,
    Do not speak of another's faults,
    Do not inquire another's affairs.

46. Stepping Forward from the Top of a Pole

Seon Master Seok Sang said, "How will you step forward from the top of a hundred-foot pole?" Another old eminent Seon Master said, "Though one who is sitting on the top of a hundred-foot pole has entered realization, it is not yet real. By all means, when he steps forward from the top of the pole, his whole body will manifest in all the ten directions."

Mu Mun's comment: If you take one more step and turn your body over, there will be no place where you are not respected. But even so, tell me, "How will you step forward from the top of a hundred-foot pole? Huh!

Verse

Making the eye on the forehead blind,
If you misread the mark on the balance,
Though you may cast aside your body and sacrifice your life,
It is like a blind man misleading other blind

men.

47. Three Barriers of Do Sol

Seon Master Do Sol (Jong) Yeol set up three barriers and asked his students,

"1) The aim of making one's way through grasses and seeking the profound truth is only to see one's own self-nature. Now, you venerable monks, in this moment, where is your self- nature?

2) If you realize self-nature, you will be free from life and death for the first time. When the light of your eyes is falling to the ground, how can you then escape from life and death?

3) If you free from birth and death, you know where to go. When your four elements disperse, Where will you go?"

Mu Mun's comment: If you can answer turning words about these three barriers, then you will be a master wherever you are, and you will give the point to them whoever you encounter. Otherwise, gulping down your food will fill you up quickly, while chewing well will make it more difficult to become hungry again.

Verse

In a single thought, looking at the kalpas widely,
The kalpas is just this moment.
If you see through this a single thought at this
moment,
You see through the one who see through it
right now.

48. One Road of Geon Bong

A monk asked Seon Master Geon Bong, "(It is written in Sutra that) 'The Bhagavat(=Buddha) of the ten directions; one road to the gate of Nirvana.' I wonder, where does that road begin?"

Seon Master Geon Bong lifted up his staff, drew a line in the air and said, "Here it is."

Later this monk went to Seon Master Un Mun and asked the same question. The Seon Master Un Mun picked up his fan and said, "This fan jumps up to the thirty-third heaven and picks the nose of King Sakra, striking the carp of the Eeastern Sea once and rain pours down like a water jar is overturned."

Mu Mun's comment: One goes the bottom of deepest sea, blows sand and raises dust. The other stands on the top of the highest mountain and makes the white waves overflow to the sky. One is holding tightly, the other is letting go. Each of them extends a single hand and supports the Seon teaching. It is just like two people running on both sides bumping into each other. There is certainly no one in the world who fully realizes the truth. When looking with the correct eye, neither of the old masters knows where the road is.

Verse

> Before even a step is taken, the goal is reached;
> Before the tongue is moved, the speech is finished.
> Though you may take the initiative, point by point,
> You must know there is still the single opening upward.

Seon Master Man Gong's Dharma Talks
The Gateless Gate

Print Date : January 29, 2021
Published Date : February 05, 2021
Publisher : Mu Cho
Editor and translator : Mu Cho
Facebook : Seon Monk Mu Cho
Publisher : Book publishing JiJangWon
Publishing Office : JiJangWon
                        Sutergol-gil 171, Yeongog-myeon,
                        Gangneung-si, South Korea, 25400
Registration Number : 282-90-01276
Registration Date : 2020. 12. 08
Tel : +82 10 5855 5009
E-mail : tothezen@gmail.com

ISBN : 979-11-973493-1-7   03220